101 EXCUSES, ALIBIS AND OBSERVATIONS
ON THE GAME OF GOLF

Published by Addax Publishing Group Inc.
Copyright © 1998 by Chuck Carlson
Designed by Randy Breeden
Cover Design by Deborah Ramirez

For information address:
Addax Publishing Group, Inc.
8643 Hauser Drive, Suite 235, Lenexa, KS 66215

ISBN: 1-886110-58-1

Distributed to the trade by Andrews McMeel Publishing
4520 Main Street
Kansas City, MO 64111

1 3 5 7 9 10 8 6 4 2

Printed in the USA

Library of Congress Cataloging-in-Publication Data

Carlson, Chuck, 1957-
        Mulligans 4 all : 101 excuses, alibis, and observations on the
    game of golf / by Chuck Carlson.
            p. cm.
        ISBN 1-886110-58-1
        1. Golf—Humor. I. Title.
    GV967.C27 1998
    796.352'02'07—dc21   98-24658
                                                            CIP

Mulligans 4 All

101 EXCUSES, ALIBIS AND OBSERVATIONS ON THE GAME OF GOLF

by Chuck Carlson

Illustrated by Brad Kirkland

ADDAX PUBLISHING GROUP

DEDICATION

To all those wonderfully, hopelessly misguided folks who really believe that, with one more lesson or one more really expensive piece of equipment, they will be ready for the PGA Tour. Keep those dreams alive.

ACKNOWLEDGEMENTS

I'd like to thank all the truly bad golfers I have played with over the years for giving me the ammunition for this handbook. It never ceases to amaze me how people can come out day after day, week after week, year after year and continue to play this game that always gets the best of them. Maybe that's what makes it so much fun.

I'd also like to thank the good golfers I have played with over the years who have put up with my bad shots and worse excuses as I butchered a perfectly splendid 18 holes.

As always, the folks at Addax Publishing have been superb. Bob Snodgrass, as usual, has pretty much left me to my own devices, assuming I wouldn't screw things up too badly.

Hopefully I haven't. Thanks again to Darcie Kidson (See! I spelled your name right), who once again has thrown just enough fear into me to get this project done on time. And there are the other folks at Addax like Sharon Snodgrass, Michelle Washington and Brad Breon who always have something nice to say even when there's nothing nice to say. I appreciate it.

Also, a big thank you to Brad Kirkland, whose illustrations can be found throughout the book. They make a big difference.

Thanks as well to my wife, Theresa, who knows as much about golf as I know about molecular physics. Yet she offered some excellent suggestions, criticism and advice that have made this a better book. I think.

– Chuck Carlson
 August, 1998

INTRODUCTION

You stand 128 yards from the green. You could not be any better positioned in the middle of the fairway if you took the ball and placed it there by hand, which, come to think of it, you considered doing.

Still coursing through your brain is the memory of that perfect, I mean perfect, tee shot you had just hit. Somehow, some way, the planets aligned and the gods smiled and you did everything mechanically you were always taught to do. Not that you have any clue what you did correctly and not that you ever expect to do it again, but on this one occasion, at this one time, it all fell together.

You took your driver back, swung your hips nicely, pivoted your feet precisely and drove through the ball with a savagery that took you back to your days in the primordial ooze millions of years ago.

The ball screamed off the tee and hurtled through the sultry morning air, landing 243 yards straight down the fairway. The fairway you're actually playing in and not the one two holes over where you usually end up. A drive so good, so lovely, so complete you can't even smile about it because then everyone would know the truth. Everyone would know that, if the devil himself had asked, you would have sold your soul for that shot.

But we digress.

There you stand, 135 yards from the hole, the ball sitting up so nicely in the impossibly green grass just begging you to hit it. There is a slight breeze blowing into your face. You know this, of course, because you reached down, grabbed a few blades of grass and threw them into the air the way you saw Arnold Palmer do it so many years ago on TV.

You take your seven-iron from the bag because it's the only iron you know you can hit with anything resembling consistency. You take your place over the ball and then it hits.

With a good second shot, you have a chance for a birdie. Not a par, which would normally make your decade, but a birdie. The Holy Grail. The thing that separates you from all the other riff-raff that plays this stupid game. A good second shot, that's all you need. Something within 15 feet or so that would allow you to use your $200 putter for something more than holding the garage door open. A birdie. That would impress everyone and, more important, give you justification for spending $3,000 on that golf vacation to Hawaii.

But you knew it wouldn't be that easy.

Suddenly the club weighs 400 pounds and the ball is the size of a microbe. The wind is hurricane force, everyone in town is watching you, your fly is open, your hair is on fire and, yes, the ball is talking to you.

"Come on," it taunts. "Let's see watcha got. "

You close your eyes and try to recall what it was that you did so well the shot before, the shot that made you think you actually knew what you were doing.

But all you can hear is the golf ball, talking to you in derisive, mocking tones.

"You got nothin'," it says. "You think you can hit me? Ha, ha. Good luck, loser. You couldn't hit me with a baseball bat. Ha, ha And your fly is open. Ha, ha."

But you try to block it out because you know with this shot, you can erase all the bad memories, all the rotten shots, all the times you swore you'd never play golf again.

The club goes back, your head is down and it feels....right.

You accelerate through your downswing, visualizing a perfect

divot, the ball lofting lazily into the air and landing nine feet from the hole. This is it and you know it.

You make contact with the ball and everything you know, everything you've dreamed about, everything that is important to you collides at the nexus.

The next moment, the ball is six yards ahead of you and a divot the size of Greenland is 10 yards ahead.

"Ha, ha, ha," the ball screeches. "Told ya. What a loser. What a moron. That's the best you can do? I know a dead guy who hits seven-irons farther than you do!! Oh this is rich, this is priceless. Oooh, I better watch out for the big bad golfer. Hey loser, has the PGA called yet?"

You stare at the ball and the anger and frustration well up inside. Again. You'd throw your club but you're way too mature for that. Besides, you'd just get kicked off the golf course again and people are starting to talk.

Instead, you take a deep breath and snap back to reality. You will not be playing in The Masters this year after all. The birdie? That lovely, long-sought birdie, the one you didn't even have to cheat to get, is all but gone. So you trudge to the ball, which isn't talking anymore, and, with nothing to lose, you whack it splendidly to within 25 feet of the flagstick.

Two putts later, you have a solid, unremarkable, uninspiring 5. Not bad, but nothing close to what you had envisioned just five minutes earlier.

You finish your round disgusted and exhilarated at the same time and you don't know why.

This game has done it to you again. This miserable, inspiring, infuriating, addicting game has taken you down the rose-covered path again only to show you it's another dead-end. And blindly you follow because you have no choice, no will, no conscious thought of your own. The game has afflicted you like a virus, it is in your bloodstream and it's not leaving.

You learned long ago what would happen the minute you picked up a golf club. You knew what you were in for. You knew what the game would do to you but, more importantly, you knew what the game could do for you. You knew golf would frustrate and anger and annoy and persecute you long after a round had ended.

But as you thought about all the miserable shots you hit and all the rotten putts and how it took you a day and a half to get out of a bunker on the seventh hole, you knew something else. You knew that you also did enough good things to keep you coming back for more. You knew that, if you kept at it, this game would begin to make sense and that, in time, you'd be the golfer you always dreamed of being.

Or not.

Let's face it, most of us will never be anything more than stunningly mediocre. Whether we don't have the time or the inclination or the equipment or the talent or any of the other three zillion reasons that separates us mere mortals from Tiger Woods, we are who we are.

We love the game, but we are also cursed with the kind of self-awareness that tells us that love will not be reciprocated any time in this lifetime.

So we plunge on, dutifully playing the game we swore we wouldn't take too seriously but do anyway. And off in the distance, we still see the player we want to be, the player for whom everything becomes so effortless, so seamless. The player who curses when his drive only goes 295 yards. The player who expects to hole a chip shot from ankle-deep rough.

We can dream, can't we?

To that end, here is your book. It contains no scientific formulas, no particular words of wisdom and offers not one clue for how to hit a three-iron.

Instead, it offers truly practical information for making this bizarre, perplexing game seem a little more sane. It probably won't take any strokes off your game but, then again, have any of those others books and gadgets and devices you spent way too much money on? Take this for what it's worth and try to remember that golf, despite everything you've heard and seen, is supposed to be fun, fun, fun.

But if your golf ball does happen to start a conversation with you, it might be time to look into another form of recreation.

Enjoy.

NO. 1

If that new pair of golf shoes costs more than your house payment, you don't need them.

NO. 1

NO. 2

If that wondrous new over-sized driver that does everything but hit golf balls where you want them to go costs more than your appendectomy, you don't need it.

NO. 3

If that golf bag, which has more pockets than a pool table costs more than your '69 Mustang, you don't need it.

NO. 4

The 10th biggest lie told about golf: "It doesn't matter what you shoot as long as you're having fun."

NO. 5

Use three balls on every hole. You have to figure one of them will work out.

NO. 6

Do away with first tee jitters and simply pick up your ball and throw it. Chances are, that's how far it's going to go if you try to hit it with the golf club anyway.

NO. 7

Count every other shot. You'll be amazed how quickly your score plummets.

NO. 6

NO. 8

Move the 19th hole up to the 18th hole.

NO. 9

Deduct a stroke from your round every time you hit a ball into a fairway other than the one you're playing on.

NO 10.

Mulligans for all. All the time. Whenever you want them. Whenever you need them. It's only a game, right?

NO. 11

Every putt is a "gimme" inside 15 feet.

NO. 12

The 10th most frequent excuse used in golf: "The wind was blowing."

NO. 13

Forbid the television networks from covering Tiger Woods anymore. Who needs to watch another young multi-gazillionaire looking annoyed when his tee shot only goes 346 yards?

NO. 14

Make the pros who produced those silly how-to videos actually try to use them.

NO. 15

Make anything ever written by Harvey Penick required reading before anyone even thinks about picking up a golf club.

NO. 16

Hold the U.S. Open at a municipal course somewhere in Wyoming. That will really be a test.

NO. 17

Fun golf facts to know and tell: In 1934, Paul Runyan was the PGA Tour's leading money winner with $6,767. Today? Greg Norman wouldn't even brush his teeth for that.

NO. 18

The 9th most frequent excuse used in golf: "I need a new putter."

IN THE BEGINNING...

A long time ago on a golf course far, far away....

He can still recall the smells, the sounds, the sublime wonder of that first trip to a golf course. He was 14 years old and thoroughly invincible. At 14, who isn't?

But as he stepped on the impossibly green grass and looked down the first fairway he'd ever seen in his life, a new feeling hit him.

What was it? Uncertainty? Sure. Anxiety? OK. Fear? Uh-oh.

There were strangers watching him as he held the golf club like it was a poisonous snake or something. He had to go up there, strike the ball and pretend as though he knew what he was doing.

This was an arena he had never been thrust into before and, for the first time in his young life, he had no idea what he'd gotten himself into. He knew baseball and football and basketball. He'd even had a passing acquaintance with soccer and tennis.

But this game was something else. This golf, which he had only watched on TV with the old man but had never played, was something else altogether.

But you are 14 and invincible and impervious to doubt. Besides, you'd watch them play on TV and how tough could it be?

You found out soon enough.

With his brand new set of golf clubs (which cost $75, bag not included), he strode to the tee, placed the ball down, took a couple of practice swings, took a deep breath and swung.

Strike one.

That is his first golf memory. Agonizing and embarrassing as it is, that was it. His first swing and the ball got a cold from the wind whipping past it as he swung right over the top of the stationary object.

He turned to his father who simply nodded.

He tried it again and the ball sailed maybe 100 yards down the fairway. It had begun.

Can anyone say they don't have a memory like this from the infancy of their game? Doubtful. Humbling and exhilarating at the same time, the earliest memories are the strongest memories and, it's funny, the bad moments are just as memorable as the good ones.

Why is that?

Anyway, the kid's first round of golf consisted of nine agonizing holes of which the final score has melted away over the years. It felt like about 153, though it probably wasn't.

But as he commiserated with the old man at the snack bar afterward, another odd feeling came over him. Though he hacked and chopped away through the course like he was in the Amazon jungle, he found he was really getting into this game.

Each shot was different, that was certain. Each shot meant imminent peril yet each shot also offered a chance for redemption, and that was reason enough to continue on.

He had never battled anything so hard in his life, yet the kid couldn't wait to come out and do it all over again.

This was fun. In some bizarre, sick way, this was an absolute blast and as they packed their clubs away for the day, the kid thanked the old man for the time of his life.

And the old man simply smiled.

The journey had begun.

NO. 19

Charge greens fees only to those golfers who can break 80.

NO. 20

Make The Masters a Pro-Am.

NO. 21

Allow every golfer one chance a round to hit the ball as far as John Daly, as straight as Ernie Els, putt as well as Ben Crenshaw and keep his wits about him like Jack Nicklaus.

NO. 22

Make Arnold Palmer golf's patron saint.

NO. 22

NO. 23

The 8th most frequent excuse used in golf: "The sun was in my eyes."

NO. 24

Hold the Ryder Cup every year, instead of every two years.

NO. 25

The 9th biggest lie told about golf: "You look great in yellow polyester slacks."

NO. 23

NO. 26

Put the word "mashie" back in golf lingo.

NO. 27

Trust no one who claims they use a swing doctor.

NO. 28

Use a head cover for your putter. It may not make a difference in how you putt, but it sure makes it look like you know what you're doing.

NO. 27

NO. 29

If, after taking golf lessons for five years, your game doesn't noticeably improve, you get your money back. Or 15 minutes alone in an empty room with your Big Bertha and the golf pro who taught you.

NO. 30

Golf balls are now being produced with titanium cores. When it gets to nuclear fusion, you may want to consider quitting.

NO. 30

NO. 31

Do something no one ever does on the course anymore and carry your clubs. It will intimidate everyone else you're playing with.

NO. 32

Deduct a month's pay from every TV analyst who insists on saying, "That was a great golf shot." What else could it be? A great tennis shot?

THAT FIRST BIRDIE

It occupies a special place in your heart. Your first car, your first love (which may actually not be your first car), your first dog, your first job, your first...oops, never mind.

And on that list of firsts — really high on that list in some cases — was that first birdie. Remember? How could you forget?

For the first time, you brought the golf course to its knees. For the first time, you played a hole under par. You got the better of it, you defeated it and you felt like you could take on the whole world.

And you didn't have to cheat. That was the best part.

It didn't matter how you got the birdie. What was important was that you did it. You did what the pros all take for granted.

On the 120-yard par 3, your tee shot landed within 10 feet of the hole and you rammed home the putt with the confidence of Jack Nicklaus in his prime.

And when you circled that on your scorecard, you felt 20 feet tall and covered in steel.

Of course, on the next hole, that pesky par-5 with the dogleg left was another story.

Still full of yourself and convinced you were on a roll, you yanked your tee shot into the trees and it took a compass, a St. Bernard and the National Guard to get you out. You finish with a solid 11 on that hole and you are returned to your place in the golfing cosmos.

Still...

The memory will linger forever of the time, for at least one hole, when you were better than it was.

NO. 33

This from Richard C. Helmstetter, Senior VP and Chief of New Products at Callaway Golf, describing his company's new oversized irons: "We did finite-element analysis and a modal analysis of the basic design." Either he's describing a golf club or a new car design.

NO. 34

The 7th most frequent excuse used in golf: "Somebody was talking during my backswing."

NO. 34

NO. 35

Find someone who really knows what a stimpmeter is.

NO. 36

Defy everyone and buy a one-iron. Don't ever use it, but buy it anyway.

NO. 37

Don't try too many practice swings. After five, you look desperate.

NO. 38

The 8th biggest lie told about golf: "Only 110 yards? Sure you can use a pitching wedge."

NO. 39

A sign posted on the Bethpage "Black Course" in Farmingdale, N.Y.: "Warning: The Black Course is an extremely difficult course which is recommended only for highly skilled golfers."

NO. 40

The 6th most frequently used excuse in golf: "These aren't my regular clubs."

NO. 41

Never use an orange ball when playing in the fall.

NO. 42

Try and convince the club you're playing at that day to use winter rules — even if it's August.

NO. 43

Get your clubs re-gripped every two years. Chewing on them really does take a toll.

NO. 44

Buy over-sized irons. You may not hit the ball any straighter but you can sure hit it out of bounds a lot farther.

NO. 43

NO. 45

The 7th biggest lie told about golf: "Just keep your head down and your left arm straight."

NO. 46

Be sure to carry flares and a snack because you never know when you'll end up in a pot bunker.

NO. 47

Bring only the number of clubs you know you'll use during a round. For most of us, that means a driver (if you're really feeling lucky), a three-wood, a five-iron, a nine-iron, a sand wedge and a putter.

THE TOOLS OF BATTLE

I picked up the $700 driver and looked at it the way the Neanderthal must have looked at the sun for the first time.

How could an instrument used in a game cost that much money? What else did it do? Cure cancer? Was it some historical or religious relic? What? What else did it do to justify that price tag?

Then I found out.

I took it to the indoor driving range and discovered what ultimate bliss and total satisfaction feel like.

So perfectly balanced, so wonderfully aligned, I took the club and I wasn't even aware of it. The club face connected with the ball and it roared into the net, making a qwonk sound signifying that the sweet spot had been found and exploited.

I stared at the club and wondered just where that ball would have ended up if I'd been on the golf course. My mind ran rampant. It would have been one of those 340-yard drives that takes fairway bunkers and dog legs out of play altogether.

The thought made my heart race.

I hit another. And another. And another. Each more perfect than the last (or so my rapidly inflating ego told me). Eventually, the salesman moved closer, watching closely to make sure I didn't try to smuggle the instrument of destruction under my shirt.

"Sir, there are other people waiting," he finally said, pointing to a line of equally pathetic people drooling over the prospect of using a club that none would ever own.

Then the thought slipped into my fevered brain. If I got a second job, took a second mortgage on my house, gave up solid food for six, well seven, months then I could perhaps afford that marvelous piece of golf weaponry.

Eventually, however, sanity returned and the realization washed over me that I could not own a golf club that cost more than my car payments. There was something intrinsically wrong with that, wasn't there?

Besides, if I owned it and still couldn't play the game worth a lick, then what excuse did I have? So I will do without until, of course, the next line of new-age clubs come a long and make this one obsolete. And the way things are going, that figures to be sometime next month.

NO. 48

Use the plumb-bob technique for lining up a putt. You may have absolutely no idea what you're doing, but it sure looks impressive.

NO. 49

Always go to the driving range before a round. If you can't hit the ball out of your shadow, go home and save the $50 in greens fees.

NO. 50

The 5th most frequently used excuse in golf: "Damn birds."

NO. 51

If you're not nervous on the first tee, you clearly don't like the game.

NO. 52

"Give the ball a good, healthy whack and enjoy yourself," Arnold Palmer said. Why is it great players can say that and it makes so much sense?

NO. 53

Understand at some point that you will never win the U.S. Open or the Masters. Understand at some point you will never shoot in the 60s (for 18 holes, that is). Understand at some point that you are playing golf for the enjoyment of it. Once you reach that perfect state of being, you will find golf not quite so intimidating.

NO. 54

Always bring a cellular phone to a golf tournament and have a friend call you when a player's in his backswing. It may not be sporting but it sure is fun.

NO. 55

Never retrieve a ball hit into an active volcano. Take the penalty stroke and move on.

NO. 56

Play at least once a month at 6 a.m. It will do wonders.

NO. 57

At least once a round, putt with your eyes closed. Could you really do any worse?

NO. 58

The 6th biggest lie told about golf: "The putt breaks just a little left."

NO. 59

Never play with a 14-year-old kid who can outdrive you by 150 yards. You've got enough aggravation.

NO. 60

On your next hole-in-one, don't gloat. Act like you expected it all the time.

NO. 61

The 4th most frequently used excuse in golf: "There was a bug on my ball."

NO. 62

If you're right-handed, never watch a left-hander play.

NO. 61

NO. 63

Once in your life, try to hit a set a $1,500 irons. It's sort of like test-driving a BMW when you drive a Saturn.

NO. 64

The main irrefutable law of golf: The less time you have to play is directly proportional to how slow the foursome ahead of you is playing.

NO. 64

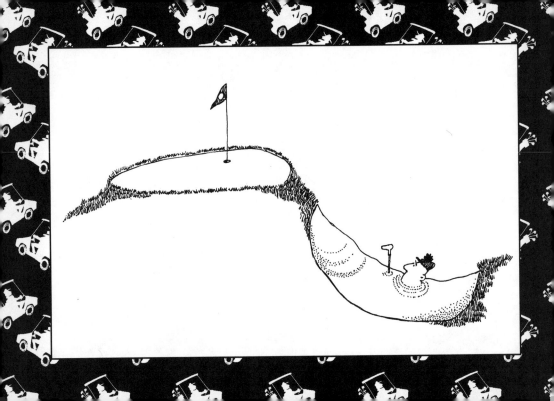

HEAVEN ON EARTH

They stand there in their pristine silence, a testament to your ultimate futility. You know it and you fight it but you also know it's like swimming against the tide. The green grass, the white sand, the gorgeous pines and the spectacular water.

Taken in a different setting, you'd call it a national park and gladly fork over $50 for a chance to go camping in it. But in this context, it's called a golf course and the journey is considerably more difficult.

It seduces you, draws you in, makes you feel that all this pastoral beauty can't be anything but therapeutic for you. Fresh air, sunshine, the illusion of exercise. And just when you're convinced that this is actually good for you, you hit your first drive into the trees.

Then you find that sand trap on the right side of the green and it takes a day and a half to get out of it. Then you tomahawk your five-wood into the lake. Then you find yourself on a first-name basis with the ankle-deep rough.

By the time you have traversed the 18 holes, you feel as though you've been through a blender. And the golf course is still there, unchanged, unfazed, totally unaware that you've ever been there.

But how can you be angry at something so beautiful, so tranquil, so perfect. From the scruffiest municipal course to the most exclusive country club, every golf course has a haunting beauty that always stays with you.

Like some unruly child, you can get angry and frustrated with a course. But you can't stay mad. And before long, you are lured back again, ready to correct the mistakes you made the last time when this piece of real estate brought you to your knees. Indeed, you learn your lesson, you make adjustments and you don't make the same mistakes you did before. You make all new ones.

But, for some strange reason, that just doesn't seem to matter because, somewhere along the line, you learned that the golf course will always win. And there's absolutely nothing wrong with that.

NO. 65

Always try the tuna fish sandwich in the club's restaurant.

NO. 66

The second irrefutable law of golf: After you hit that perfect draw shot around the tree and 12 feet from the cup, you won't know how you did it and, worse, you realize no one was watching as you did it.

NO. 67

The third irrefutable law of golf: Just when you get in a routine of playing three times a week and watching your score shrink, you break your leg.

NO. 68

Don't worry about sidehill lies. You can hit those shots just as badly as any other.

NO. 69

The 5th biggest lie told about golf: "A bunker shot is no different than any other."

NO. 70

The 3rd most frequently used excuse in golf: "I usually hit a three-wood much better than that."

NO. 71

A rule of thumb when shooting toward a green you can't see. If you hear the sound of someone screaming or glass breaking, chances are you won't like where you ended up.

NO. 72

Teach your kid to play golf at age 6. That way, when he makes the PGA Tour 20 years later, he can take care of you in your old age.

NO. 73

Refrain from saying, "That would have been a good shot if it was straight," more than three times a round.

NO. 74

If your head says lay up and your heart says go for the green, always listen to your head. Or your heart.

NO. 75

"What a beautiful place a golf course is. From the meanest country pasture to the Pebble Beaches and St. Andrews of the world, a golf course to me is a holy ground. I feel God in the trees and grass and flowers, in the rabbits and the birds and the squirrels, in the sky and in the water. I feel that I am home."

— *Golf guru Harvey Penick*

NO. 76

Choose a swing that's comfortable for you. If it works, well, you're one of the lucky ones.

NO. 77

The final irrefutable law of golf: On the one hole you're certain you can't reach the water hazard, that's the one hole you'll hit the drive of your life.

NO. 78

Always replace your divots. You may not be any good but, by Gosh, you are neat.

NO. 76

NO. 79

The 4th biggest lie told about golf: "You can hit it between those branches. No really, you can."

NO. 80

Always over-tip your caddy — even if you played rotten. They have lives too, you know.

NO. 79

LEARNING A LESSON

There is a rare breed out there who can pick up a golf club and automatically know what to do with it.

Some call them "natural athletes." Some call them "gifted." Some call them something far worse than that. But they do exist and you have learned (or at least tried) to live with it. You watch with anger, envy and awe as someone who wouldn't know a mashie from a niblick takes a flawless, impeccable swing and knocks the ball far too straight.

No lessons, no training, nothing. Just grab the club and whack it.

For some people, it is that easy.

But not for you, Oh no. Not at all.

For you, lessons are the order of the day, the month and the year. You have taken so many golf lessons you feel you can start teaching them yourself. But, unfortunately, despite all the teaching, there is a part of your brain that just can't make the connection. You know what you're supposed to do, or at least you think you do. But the connection is never made and you hack away earnestly, but hopelessly.

That's when you realize that, unless you're one of those disgusting "gifted" types, you could probably stand to take a lesson or two from someone who knows what they're doing.

The intent of golf lessons is a noble one, to be sure. The professional seems to genuinely want to see a duffer like you improve his game. And for many, lessons open a whole new world.

Ah, but for others, they are nothing but a serious pain in the neck.

It's especially awkward for someone who has played golf for years, discovered they stink and then decide to take lessons. By that point, though, too many bad habits have been ingrained and they are next to impossible to break.

Little things, like the grip and how to stand, come under attack. The teacher, hoping to convince a player a change is needed, gets frustrated. The student, convinced the teacher is some sadistic creep, digs in his heels and wont change.

Everyone gets frustrated and nothing gets accomplished. It becomes obvious at that point that for some, golf lessons are about as useful as roller skates on a hippo.

It also becomes obvious that, just maybe, lessons aren't right for some people. You tried, it didn't work and now it's time to go back to doing whatever it was you were doing before.

It may not be pretty. It certainly isn't effective. But it is your own special way, it makes you reasonably happy and maybe that's all that matters.

NO. 81

When all else fails, follow the creed of John Daly and simply "Grip it and rip it." What could it hurt?

NO. 82

The 2nd most frequently used excuse in golf: "I left my wallet at home."

NO. 83

Fun golf fact to know and tell: In 1997, 1,200 players entered the PGA Tour qualifying school. Fewer than 60 scored well enough to play on Tour the next year.

NO. 84

Put airbags on golf carts. Just in case.

NO. 85

Do not try to explain to a non-golfer how a wood could be made of metal and still be called a wood.

NO. 86

Do not play a "Skins" game with anyone who's custom-designed balls have a skull and crossbones logo on them.

NO. 87

If your golf equipment contains more space-age materials than the Space Shuttle, then you are running out of excuses for being lousy.

NO. 88

The 3rd biggest lie told about golf: "Any moron can hit out of a divot."

NO. 89

Quit if your golf ball starts talking to you.

NO. 90

Ignore the advice of anyone who uses a paper sack for a golf bag.

NO. 91

Accept the advice of anyone who knows what the phrase "knock-down three-iron" really means.

NO. 92

Ignore the advice of anyone who says "Caddy Shack" was the best golf movie ever.

NO. 93

Accept the advice of anyone who says "Tin Cup" was the best golf movie ever.

NO. 94

Put on retainer anyone who says Dan Jenkins' "Dead Solid Perfect" was the best golf book ever written.

NO. 95

The 2nd biggest lie told about golf: "That new $2,000 set of gold-plated clubs will shave 10 strokes off your game."

NO. 96

Available for a mere $12,000 is an inch tall platinum-mounted pendant that holds .88 carats of round and baguette-cut diamonds arranged like stars in a constellation. And you thought you needed help with your short game.

NO. 95

NO, PLEASE, YOU FIRST

Perhaps no game is so steeped in proper etiquette than golf.

By the time you memorize all the things you shouldn't do on the course, you've forgotten what it is you can do.

The list is too long to cover here, but we can at least touch on some of the bigger do's and don'ts in the game.

First and foremost, never talk while another player is hitting. Never. Never. Never. You could embezzle the country club's funds and be more accepted than if you had a reputation for talking during someone's backswing.

It has never been adequately explained to me why this is such a heinous crime. Athletes in every other sport have to compete with screaming, volatile, obnoxious fans and other ear-splitting noises. But if a twig cracks three fairways over, you will never fail to see to a pro step away from his shot, glare angrily at the noise and attempt to compose himself again.

It's just as bad on our level. If you talk, thus breaking a player's concentration and forcing him to chunk his nine-iron, you are an insensitive lout raised in a barn somewhere. Never mind that the offended player had chunked his nine-irons all day, you were responsible for this one.

So, keep your mouth shut.

Second, if you shot a 12 on the par-3 ninth hole, you'd better write down a 12 on your scorecard because someone, somewhere will know if you don't.

It's amazing. You could spend an entire day playing golf with your buddies and none of them will remember anything. But every one knows if you try to cheat.

So, be honest. It's just a game for crying out loud.

And third, never hit into the foursome ahead of you — especially if it's a group of old ladies.

Nothing enrages a golfer more than preparing to hit a shot and watching an alien Titleist roll up next to you.

The proper response to this intrusion? You could ignore it, but then you leave yourself open to more of it. You could also grind the ball into the ground, throw it back at the offending player or, my favorite, simply take the ball.

That way, when the offending players comes looking for his ball, he not only will think he's too stupid to keep track of where he hit it, but he'll also have to take a stroke for a lost ball.

It's petty and childish, perhaps, but it serves a purpose.

Now, if you're the one that hit the ball into the foursome ahead, there is only recourse — look away and blame somebody else.

Last on the list of etiquette, always compliment somebody else's shot. Trust me on this.

Even if it's not that great a shot, try to come up with a "Good shot from there."

If nothing else, your playing partners will think you're a classy person and, besides, they'll probably say the same thing to you when you hit a crappy shot.

NO. 97

Force everyone who plays golf to play — just once in their lives — in Scotland.

NO. 98

The most frequently used excuse in golf: "If I only played more often..."

NO. 99

Make world-renowned course designer Pete Dye explain what connections his ancestors had with the Spanish Inquisition.

NO. 100

The biggest lie told about golf: "This is great exercise."

NO. 101

Try a less stressful activity, like juggling chainsaws or disarming land mines.

NO. 101

Chuck Carlson has been a writer since age 15, stringing high school football games for local newspapers. He is the author of *Puck! Kirby Puckett: Baseball's Last Warrior* and *Titletown Again: The Super Bowl Season of the 1996 Green Bay Packers*. For the past 10 years he has covered the Green Bay Packers for *The Post-Crescent* in Appleton, Wisconsin.

Other Addax Sports-Humor Books

Jockularity: The Sports Cartoons of Brad Kirkland - Volume 1
Applying the principle that nothing is so good that it can't be
laughed at, *Jockularity* offers a collection of sports cartoons
lampooning just about every facet of every sport. 144 pages.
Black and white illustrations throughout. Retail price $10.95.

**It's 3rd & Long, So... 101 Ways to Improve the Game of Football
by Clay Latimer**
This humorous book proposes 101 ways to improve football.
Some are cynical, some fanciful, some radical - and none has a
shot at being enacted until Tampa Bay freezes over. Hilarious
cartoons highlight the action. Hardcover, 144 pages. More than
35 black and white illustrations. Retail price $9.95.

To order individual or bulk copies of
these books please contact.
Addax Publishing Group, Inc.
8643 Hauser Drive, Suite 235
Lenexa, KS 66215
1-800-598-5550